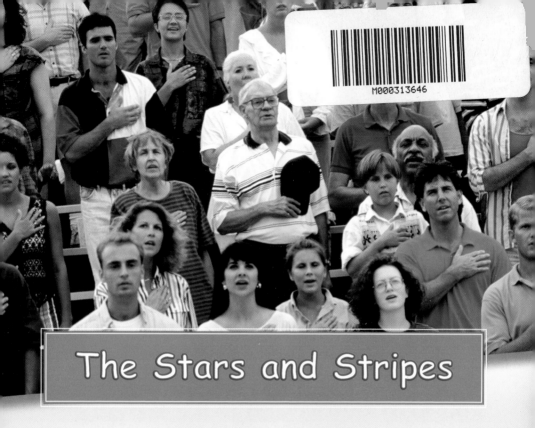

The Stars and Stripes

by Melissa Valdez

PEARSON

Scott
Foresman

Editorial Offices: Glenview, Illinois • Parsippany, New Jersey • New York, New York
Sales Offices: Needham, Massachusetts • Duluth, Georgia • Glenview, Illinois
Coppell, Texas • Sacramento, California • Mesa, Arizona

Think about a parade. Someone marches by with the American flag, and everyone stands. People take off their hats. Many people put their hands over their hearts. Why do they do these things?

People show honor to the flag and to the United States when they do these things.

---

honor: respect

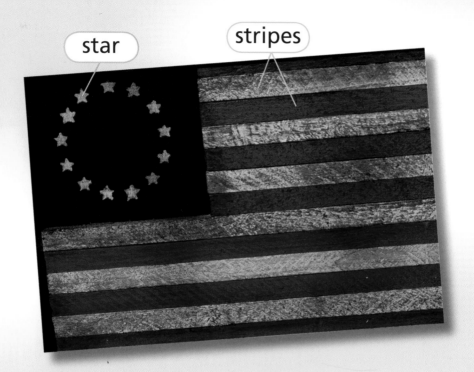

star

stripes

The First Flags

The American flag has not always looked the way it does today. The United States has changed. So has the American flag!

When the United States was a new country, there were 13 states. The first American flag had 13 stars and 13 stripes. The stars and stripes stood for the first states of the country.

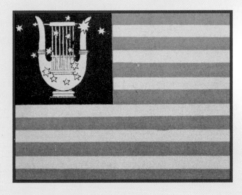

Early flags did not always look the same.

Over the years, the flag changed. More states joined the country. More stars and stripes were added to the flag. But the stars and stripes did not look the same on every flag. The stars were placed in different ways. Some stars even had a different number of points. Flag makers sometimes made the stripes look different, too.

Pledge to the Flag

In 1892, Francis Bellamy wrote a pledge, or promise, to the flag. It is called the *Pledge of Allegiance*. The pledge was first printed in a magazine for young people. School children all across the country began to say the pledge everyday.

Many children still say the pledge today. Saying the pledge is another way to honor the flag and America.

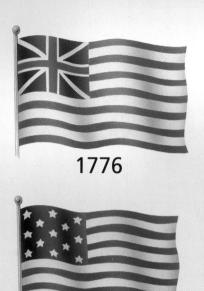

1776

1777

1777

1776

One Flag for Everyone

In 1912, President Taft said that all United States flags had to look the same. Each flag needed 13 stripes. There should be a star for every state. The stars should be in rows.

---

rows: straight lines

flagpole

The Flag Today

The American flag has 13 stripes. The stripes stand for the first states of the country. The flag has 50 stars. These stars stand for each state in the United States. Sometimes our flag is called "The Stars and Stripes."

Where do you see the flag? Today schools have American flags that fly overhead. You can also see the flag in front of other public buildings, such as libraries and fire stations. Parks and sports fields have flags, too.

When you see the flag, think about how our country has grown. The Stars and Stripes will help you remember!